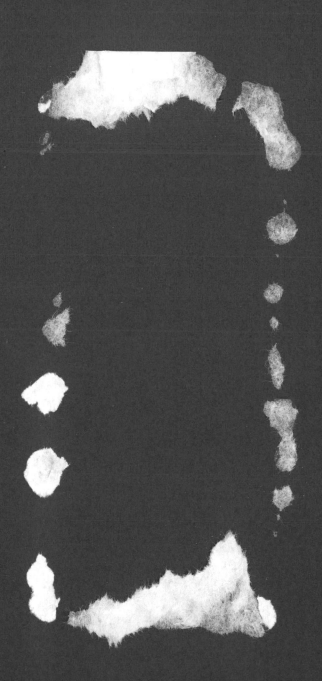

# THE GIRAFFE THAT WALKED TO PARIS

by NANCY MILTON

illustrated by ROGER ROTH

CROWN PUBLISHERS, INC., NEW YORK

This is the true story of

a wonderful giraffe

that lived a long time ago.

She was young

and beautiful,

and she belonged to

the pasha of Egypt.

*In the year 1826,*
there had been a disagreement between Egypt and France.

"What can I do," the pasha wondered, "so that the French people and the Egyptian people will be friends?"

"I know what you can do," the French ambassador told him. "You can give the king of France a present."

"What do you think he'd like?" the pasha asked.

The ambassador thought very carefully and then replied, "I think he'd like a giraffe. The people of France have never seen one."

"That's an excellent idea," the pasha said. "I'll send him my beautiful giraffe right away."

The shortest way to travel from Egypt to France was to sail from one side of the Mediterranean Sea to the other.

"We'll need a ship," said the ambassador.

The ambassador's helpers found a good ship named *The Two Brothers* with a captain who was very pleased to take the giraffe to France.

"I'll take care of her as if she were my own daughter," he said.

Even though the giraffe was eleven feet tall, she was still a baby. Every day she drank three or four big bucketsful of milk.

"I can see we're going to need a cow," the ambassador said.

Actually they needed three cows and a person to milk them as well.

"I think the best person to milk the cows and take care of the giraffe is my Egyptian stableman, Hassan," the ambassador said. "He knows a lot about animals."

But one man wasn't enough, so Hassan found two helpers named Atir and Youssef.

When the ambassador saw that there was still some room on the ship, he decided he'd like to send a present to the king too. Knowing that the king liked African animals, he asked Hassan if he could find another interesting one. Hassan found a beautiful big antelope.

On a clear October day the giraffe, the cows, and the antelope were all in their places in the hold of the ship. The giraffe was lucky. She could see everything because her long neck stuck up through the hole that had been cut in the deck. There was straw padding around the sides so she wouldn't get bumped and a big canvas over her head so she wouldn't get too much sun or rain.

"Good-bye," the ambassador called as he waved from the dock. "Bon voyage, dear giraffe."

The wind puffed out the white sails, the flags of France and Egypt flew from the mast, and *The Two Brothers* sailed out into the Mediterranean Sea.

It was a fine trip. The only bad thing that happened was that one cow got seasick.

In late October the ship sailed into the port of Marseilles, France.

In Paris, King Charles X was very excited to hear the news.

"Wonderful," he said. "My giraffe is in France. I can't wait to see her." For the king, like the rest of the French people, had never seen a real giraffe. "When will she arrive? I hope it will be in time for Christmas."

The king's counselor was worried. He knew that kings could be quite difficult.

"Your Majesty," he said politely. "Giraffes are used to hot weather. You know how cold it gets here in the winter."

"Yes, of course I know," the king replied impatiently.

"Marseilles is in the south of France," the counselor said carefully. "It's warmer there in the winter. Perhaps it would be better..."

The king looked unhappy. "You think the giraffe should spend the winter in Marseilles."

"Yes, Your Majesty," the counselor replied, "and come to Paris in the spring when the weather is warmer."

The king sighed, but he knew the counselor was right. "I won't be able to see my wonderful present for such a long time," he said sadly.

The counselor wanted to make the king feel better, so he found a famous Paris scientist to draw a picture of a giraffe for the king.

The scientist had never seen a real giraffe either.
But the king was very pleased with the picture.

The giraffe was very popular in Marseilles. Schoolchildren came with their teachers to visit her. Professors studied her. Newspapers printed stories about her. Everyone wanted to see the strange animal with the long neck.

Every day exactly at noon the big gates of the courtyard where she lived swung open, and La Girafe, as she was called in France, walked out into the street. The sidewalks were always crowded with people waiting to see her.

"Be careful. Get out of the way!" the policemen shouted. "The giraffe is coming. The giraffe is coming."

All through the winter the giraffe went walking every day, and the people never got tired of seeing her.

At last spring came. In Paris the king looked out the window and saw new green leaves and pink and yellow flowers in his garden.

"I want to see my giraffe," he said. "I've waited a very long time for my present."

"Yes, Your Majesty," the counselor said nervously. "I'm sure the giraffe will arrive soon."

But the counselor was worried, for he had received letters from Marseilles, and he knew it wouldn't be easy to get the giraffe to Paris.

The men in Marseilles couldn't decide what to do. La Girafe was much too tall to be put in a wagon or a carriage. She had already taken a long boat trip and might not enjoy another one.

Finally Hassan had an idea. "She's a very good walker," he said. "She's had lots of exercise every day. Maybe she could walk to Paris."

What an excellent idea! Everyone was very happy.

But then there was another problem. "Who will lead her there? After all, she's going to Paris to meet the king of France. She must be led by a Frenchman—and it must be one who knows something about giraffes."

Everyone was silent. There weren't many Frenchmen who knew anything about giraffes.

But in Paris there was one, a professor who had been to Egypt.

Professor Saint-Hilaire was old and his health wasn't very good, but when he heard that someone was needed to lead the giraffe to Paris, he was very excited. He jumped up and said, "Yes! Yes! I'll go to Marseilles and bring La Girafe back here to the king."

He packed a bag, hopped into a stagecoach, and in six and a half days he met the giraffe.

Professor Saint-Hilaire had a big job getting everything ready for the journey to Paris.

The cows could walk with the giraffe. But the antelope was very big and very dangerous. It wouldn't walk quietly along the road like the giraffe and the cows.

"We'll need a strong cage for that antelope," the professor said. "We'll need a coach to carry the cage and a man to drive the coach."

And then he said, "The giraffe needs a raincoat. She's used to the hot sun, but she isn't used to wind and rain, and it rains a lot in France in the spring."

It isn't easy to make a raincoat for a giraffe, but Professor Saint-Hilaire designed a good one that covered her whole body and buttoned down the front. It even had a hood to keep her head and long neck dry.

Finally on a rainy morning in May the big procession left Marseilles. High above everyone else there was La Girafe, looking very handsome in her new raincoat. Then there were the cows, the professor in his carriage, Hassan, Atir, Youssef, and a translator to help the men understand each other's languages. There were soldiers who rode ahead to tell everyone they were coming. And last of all, there was the coach pulled by a horse and loaded with bags and sacks and the dangerous antelope in its strong cage.

In Paris the king was pacing up and down the long halls of his castle.

"It's almost the beginning of summer," he said to his counselor. "Where is my giraffe?"

"Your giraffe is walking to Paris, Your Majesty. I'm sure she's walking as fast as she can." But the counselor was still worried, for truthfully, he had no idea how fast a giraffe could walk.

The procession to Paris was a great success. Everywhere people were waiting to welcome the giraffe. They talked

about her and wrote letters to their aunts and uncles and
grandmothers and grandfathers. They said, "We saw La Girafe.
She's as tall as a house. She has the longest neck you've ever
seen. You must see her too."

So as La Girafe and her procession got closer to Paris, more
and more people crowded the roads and the towns. They named
streets after her. They put pictures of her on the signboards
of bakeries and restaurants, hotels and grocery stores. Soon
there were giraffe pictures in every town she'd walked through.

Professor Saint-Hilaire wrote reports and sent them to the king. The counselor read them aloud.

"His Majesty's giraffe is in excellent health. She has a sweet and gentle nature. The people of France love her."

"That's all very well," the king said. "But when am I going to see her?"

"The professor says that La Girafe should arrive by the end of June. All of Paris is getting ready to greet her then."

"The giraffe is my present," the king said. "But I'll be the last person in Paris to see her. That's not fair. I want to go with everyone else to welcome her."

The counselor gasped. "But Your Majesty, that's impossible. A king can't just do whatever he wants to do. The present comes to the king. The king doesn't go to the present!"

When the procession reached the outskirts of Paris, everyone in the whole city wanted to go out and meet the king's giraffe. They went in wagons, in coaches, and in boats on the river. They took along picnic lunches so they could have a "giraffe party."

"The giraffe is here! The giraffe is here!" they shouted.

It was a very exciting day. But the king wasn't there. He had to stay at home in his castle.

At five P.M. on June 30, 1827, Professor Saint-Hilaire led the giraffe into her new home: a yard in the Paris zoo. It had taken the procession forty-one days to walk from Marseilles.

"Good-bye, La Girafe," he said. "Good-bye, good-bye." He waved to the cows and the antelope, to Hassan, Atir, Youssef, the coach driver, and the translator. "I'm exhausted. I'm going home."

But no sooner had the professor collapsed into his comfortable old armchair than a messenger knocked on his door.

"The king is waiting to see his giraffe," the messenger said. "He wants you to bring her as soon as you can."

"Oh, dear, oh, dear," the tired professor thought. They couldn't just deliver La Girafe to the king's back door. By now she was famous all over Paris, and all the important people of the city wanted to see her. There had to be a proper ceremony. It would take a lot of work to get everything ready.

But at last the great day came. On July 9, a wonderful parade marched along the river Seine to the king's castle at Saint-Cloud.

There were soldiers in splendid uniforms wearing tall hats with feather plumes on top. There were professors in long robes of purple and red and green with white fur collars. There were horses dancing and prancing and carrying generals on their backs.

La Girafe was dressed up too. On her back she wore a blanket beautifully decorated with the signs of the kings of France and Egypt. Hassan, Atir, and Youssef led her proudly. And Professor Saint-Hilaire, wearing his best clothes, walked happily in front of her.

When the parade reached the garden of the king's castle, everyone lined up, with the giraffe in the most important place of all. The big doors of the castle opened, and out walked King Charles.

He couldn't believe his eyes. The spotted animal that stood in front of him was as tall as a building. Her neck was much, much longer than the one in his picture. But he tried not to look surprised.

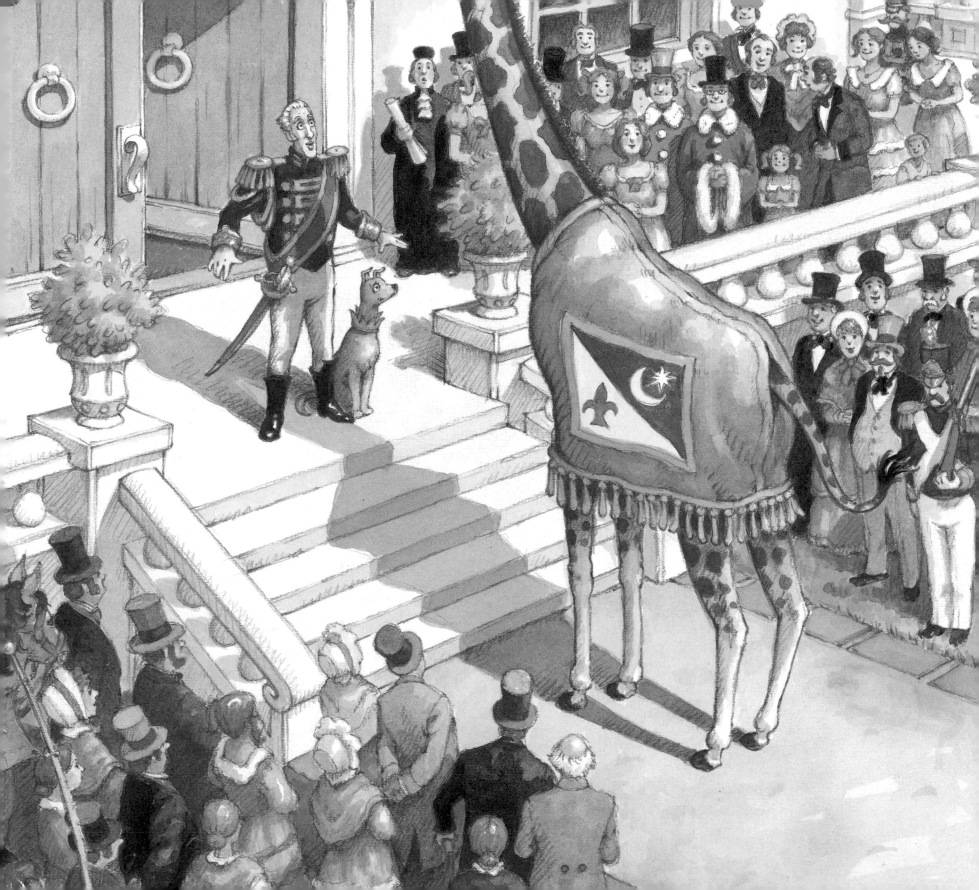

"Did you have a pleasant trip?" he asked Professor Saint-Hilaire politely.

"Yes, thank you, Your Majesty," the professor replied. "Your giraffe is a very good animal. Would you like to see her walk?"

"Yes, I would," the king said.

Hassan, Atir, and Youssef led the giraffe around the big green lawn.

"Why, look at that," the king said. "First she swings both of her right legs and then she swings both of her left legs. That's not what my horses do."

"Oh, she's very different from a horse," Professor Saint-Hilaire said. "She has a short body and long legs. If she didn't walk that way, her back feet would step on her front feet."

The king laughed. He was very pleased with his new giraffe. He'd never imagined that there could be such a strange creature in the whole world.

The king came close to the giraffe. In his hand he held the petals of a red rose.

"Here you are, my giraffe," he said. "Try these. I think you'll like them."

It is difficult for a giraffe to bend down. But La Girafe could see that the king had something good to eat in his hand, so she spread her front legs wide apart and lowered her neck. She ate the rose petals from the king's own hand.

And while her head was low enough to reach, the king's daughter-in-law put a garland of flowers around her neck and his two grandchildren petted her carefully.

"The lion may be the king of the animals," King Charles said happily, "but my giraffe is certainly the queen."

What a beautiful giraffe!

What a wonderful day!

When it was over, La Girafe went back to her new home at the zoo. Hassan and Youssef returned to Egypt, but Atir stayed to take care of the giraffe. Professor Saint-Hilaire and his friends had a special room made for them in a big glass building in the middle of the zoo. There was a stove to keep the giraffe warm in cold weather and doors that opened to let her outside when the weather was nice. Every night Atir climbed two ladders to get to his bed high up near La Girafe's head. And every day he fed her and brushed her and took her for a walk.

The people of Paris loved the giraffe very much. Thousands of them came to visit her. They put her picture on dresses and shirts and purses and on plates and cups and coffeepots. Women wore their hair in a new style—very tall like the giraffe. And when children went to the zoo to see the real giraffe, they bought gingerbread giraffes and ate them all up.

That was a long time ago. But even today, when French people visit the zoo where the king's giraffe lived and the gardens where she took her walks with Atir, they still remember her.

• SINGE •

$\mathcal{T}$HIS STORY IS BASED on real events and real people. The zoo in the Jardin des Plantes on the Left Bank of the river Seine in Paris is still in the same place it was when La Girafe lived there. When she arrived in 1827, a public zoo—or *ménagerie*, as it is called in France—was still a new idea. Until the French Revolution of 1789, the only zoos in France had been private ones at the castles of kings and nobles. But after the revolution, the animals were taken from the royal *ménagerie* at Versailles and other zoos and put in the Jardin des Plantes so that everyone could come and enjoy looking at them. But there was no giraffe.

There had never been a giraffe in France. In fact, there hadn't been one in all of Europe since the Italian nobleman Lorenzo de' Medici had had one brought to Florence, Italy, in 1486. The French royal family had been very envious of the Medici's giraffe and had tried to exchange something for it, but the Medici were not interested.

Three hundred years went by. In 1798 Napoleon Bonaparte led a military expedition to Egypt. French scholars became very interested in Egyptian subjects, and French naturalists and zoologists were fascinated by the African animals seen in Egypt, particularly the giraffes. They studied drawings of the strange creature, but few had seen a live one, and there was still no giraffe in France.

So it's not surprising that in 1827 when the pasha of Egypt, Muhammad Ali, wished to send a gift to King Charles X of France, the French ambassador to Egypt suggested that a giraffe would be very much appreciated.

At that time there was a disagreement between France and Egypt concerning another country, Greece. Greece was governed by Turkey, but the Greek people were fighting very hard for their independence. Egypt was helping Turkey by sending its army and navy to fight against the Greeks. Many people in France were angry about this, for they sympathized with the Greek struggle for independence. Muhammad Ali believed that his gift of a giraffe to King Charles X would help bring about better relations between Egypt and France.

King Charles X was said to have been a pleasant man, but he was not a good king. The youngest brother of King Louis XVI, he had grown up as a spoiled child in the court of Versailles before the French Revolution. The revolution changed France profoundly, but Charles never understood that. When he became king in 1824, he still believed a king could rule in much the same old way. He thought the king could control the newspapers and decide who should be elected to the government and which people should be allowed to vote. But the French people did not agree that the king should have so much power. In 1830 the people of Paris took to the streets and overthrew King Charles X. He and his family left France and went to live in Scotland.

So La Girafe, who had come to Paris as a gift for the king, lived there long after he had been forced to leave. When people began to lose interest in the giraffe and she was alone much of the time, Professor Saint-Hilaire and his fellow scientists started looking for a companion for her. In 1838 a young female giraffe was brought to the Jardin des Plantes by the same route that the first giraffe had traveled—from her birthplace in the Sudan to Egypt, then to Marseilles and Paris.

The two appeared to be affectionate companions and remained together until the beginning of 1845 when "The King's Giraffe" died of an undiagnosed illness from which she had

The Journey of *La Girafe*, 1826–27

By sea, about 1,700 miles

On foot, about 425 miles

suffered during her last Paris winter. She was then twenty-one years old and had lived in captivity for eighteen years. She was stuffed and kept for many years in the Museum of Natural History in Paris. Finally her remains were transferred to a museum in La Rochelle on the west coast of France, where they are still displayed today.

Text copyright © 1992 by Nancy Milton
Illustrations copyright © 1992 by Roger Roth

All rights reserved. No part of this book may be reproduced or transmitted in any form or by any means, electronic or mechanical, including photocopying, recording, or by any information storage and retrieval system, without permission in writing from the publisher. Published by Crown Publishers, Inc., a Random House company, 225 Park Avenue South, New York, New York 10003
CROWN is a trademark of Crown Publishers, Inc.
Manufactured in Singapore.
Library of Congress Cataloging-in-Publication Data
Milton, Nancy, 1929–
    The giraffe that walked to Paris / Nancy Milton ; illustrated by Roger Roth.
      p.  cm.
    Summary: Retells the true story of how the first giraffe ever to come to Europe was sent by the Pasha of Egypt to the King of France in 1826, and the giraffe walked from the disembarkation point of Marseilles to Paris to see the King.
    1. Giraffes—France—History—19th century—Juvenile literature. 2. Animal introduction—France—History—19th century—Juvenile literature. [1. Giraffes. 2. France—History—19th century.] I. Roth Roger, ill. II. Title.
QL737.U56M55  1992
599.73'57—dc20                      91-31767
ISBN 0-517-58132-9 (trade)
      0-517-58133-7 (lib. bdg.)
10 9 8 7 6 5 4 3 2 1
First Edition